DEADLY LIZARDS

PowerKiDS
press
New York

Shane McFee

Published in 2008 by The Rosen Publishing Group, Inc.
29 East 21st Street, New York, NY 10010

First Edition

Editor: Jennifer Way
Book Design: Kate Laczynski
Photo Researcher: Nicole Pristash

Photo Credits: Cover, pp. 1, 21 © Tim Flach/Getty Images; p. 5 © Paul Berquist; pp. 7, 11, 15 © Shutterstock.com; pp. 9, 13, 17, 19 © SuperStock, Inc.

Library of Congress Cataloging-in-Publication Data

McFee, Shane.
    Deadly lizards / Shane McFee. — 1st ed.
        p. cm. — (Poison!)
    Includes index.
    ISBN-13: 978-1-4042-3796-4 (lib. bdg.)
    ISBN-10: 1-4042-3796-8 (lib. bdg.)
    1. Lizards—Juvenile literature. I. Title.
    QL666.L2M374 2008
    597.95'165—dc22

                                                                2006102299

Manufactured in the United States of America

CONTENTS

Lizards! 4
Reptiles 6
The Beaded-Lizard Family........................8
Some Like It Hot 10
Underground 12
Happy Hunting..14
Chewing Up Food 16
Hatchlings 18
Lizards in Trouble...................................20
Leave Them Alone 22
Glossary 23
Index 24
Web Sites..24

LiZARDS !

Have you ever seen a lizard? You may have seen one at the zoo or on television. Most lizards are shy and will not hurt you. Did you know that some lizards have poisonous bites?

The Gila monster and the Mexican beaded lizard are two of the biggest **venomous** lizards in the world. Other lizards have venom, but only these two lizards have venom that is dangerous to people. What should you do if you see these dangerous lizards? This book will tell you.

This is a Gila monster. Gila monsters are black with yellow, orange, or pink markings.

REPTILES

Lizards are reptiles. Reptiles are cold blooded. This means the **temperature** of their blood rises and falls with the temperature of their surroundings. If a reptile is in a cold area, its blood will also be cold. Most reptiles lay eggs.

A reptile's skin is made up of scales. Scales are the thin, dry pieces of skin that form the outer covering of a lizard's body.

Other reptiles include snakes and turtles. Lizards have a lot in common with snakes. Most lizards use their tongues for smelling, like snakes do. This is why you often see lizards and snakes flicking their tongues.

This is a garter snake, which is also a reptile. When cold-blooded animals, such as reptiles, are cold, they move more slowly than they would if they were warm.

THE BEADED-LIZARD FAMILY

The Gila monster and the Mexican beaded lizard have a lot in common. They are members of the same **family**. Their family is called Helodermatidae.

These two members of the Helodermatidae family are venomous beaded lizards. They are called beaded lizards because their scales look round, like beads.

The Gila monster gets its name from the Gila River, in Arizona and New Mexico. It is called monster because it looks like a monster. These two lizards are the two **species** that make up the Helodermatidae family.

Up close, it is easy to see how the Helodermatidae lizards became known as beaded lizards. The name Helodermatidae comes from Latin words that mean "wart skin." A wart is a bumpy growth on skin.

SOME LIKE IT HOT

Most lizards live in warm **habitats**. This is because lizards are cold blooded. Remember, a lizard in a warm place has warmer blood than a lizard in a cold place.

Many lizards like to keep their skin dry at all times. This is why several species of lizards live in the desert.

Both the Mexican beaded lizard and the Gila monster live in deserts. The Mexican beaded lizard lives in Mexico and Guatemala. The Gila monster lives in Mexico and the southwestern United States. These places are warm, dry, and sunny for most of the year.

Beaded lizards like desert habitats, like the one shown here. Deserts get little rain and are warm year-round. They also are home to the small animals that these lizards eat.

11

UNDERGROUND

Most lizards dig **burrows**. The Mexican beaded lizard and the Gila monster are nocturnal. This means that they sleep in their burrows during the day and come out at night.

Burrows are warm places for lizards to **hibernate**. Although winters where these lizards live are not very cold, they are cool enough to make these cold-blooded animals' bodies slow down. Hibernating lets the lizard safely rest and wait out the cool weather.

Burrows are also good places for lizards to hide from **predators**. Coyotes eat both the Gila monster and the Mexican beaded lizard. Large birds, like eagles and hawks, eat them as well.

This Gila monster has made its burrow in the bottom of a cactus. Beaded lizards have sharp, curved claws that are good for digging holes.

HAPPY HUNTING

The lizards of the Helodermatidae family are carnivores. This means they prey on, or eat, other animals. Many small lizards eat bugs. The Gila monster and the Mexican beaded lizard are too large to live on bugs. The Gila monster can grow up to 2 feet (61 cm) long. The Mexican beaded lizard is about 3 feet (1 m) long.

The Gila monster and the Mexican beaded lizard eat birds, rodents, smaller reptiles, and the eggs of other animals. These lizards might move slowly a lot of the time, but they can move quickly when they are hungry!

Prairie dogs, like the one shown here, are small desert rodents. They make a nice meal for Gila monsters and Mexican beaded lizards! When there is no food around, beaded lizards can live off the fat in their tails!

CHEWING UP FOOD

A lizard does not use its venom the same way a snake does. A snake bites its prey once to let out enough poison to kill it. Lizard venom is not strong enough to do that.

A lizard makes venom with special **glands** in its mouth. The venom mixes with the lizard's **saliva**. The lizard must chew its prey in order to let out enough venom to poison it.

The Gila monster and the Mexican beaded lizard also use their venom when they need to **defend** themselves. These lizards have very strong jaws, or mouthparts. They bite down hard and will hold on for a long time.

This is a Mexican beaded lizard. Its venom glands are in its lower jaw. Small but sharp teeth let it hold on tight so the venom can flow into a bite.

HATCHLINGS

Every spring, Helodermatidae lizards **mate**. The females lay as many as 13 eggs. The mother buries her eggs in the desert sand. Unlike most mothers, the female lizard does not stay with the eggs. She leaves them in their hiding place. This is so they will be safe and warm, but sometimes other animals will eat the lizard's eggs.

The eggs will hatch, or break open, by the end of the summer. Baby lizards are called hatchlings. If they are lucky, the hatchlings will live for a long time. Gila monsters can live up to 20 years. Mexican beaded lizards can live over 30 years.

This is a Mexican beaded lizard hatchling. Hatchlings are about 3 to 5 inches (8–13 cm) long. Adults are around 2 feet (61 cm) long.

LIZARDS IN TROUBLE

The Gila monster and the Mexican beaded lizard can hurt people. Humans can also hurt them. People hunt these lizards because they are afraid of their venom. People have also destroyed the lizards' habitat by building homes and roads in places where these lizards live.

There are not very many Gila monsters or Mexican beaded lizards left. Both lizards are almost **endangered**. It is now against the law to hurt them.

Even though they are dangerous, these lizards are helpful in many different ways. They eat rodents and other pests, which helps control their numbers. Scientists have studied Gila monster saliva to make drugs for people with diabetes.

Hopefully, the laws that make it illegal to harm beaded lizards will help keep them from becoming endangered.

LEAVE THEM ALONE !

The Gila monster and the Mexican beaded lizard are not **aggressive**. This means they will never attack humans unless they think they are in danger and cannot run away and hide. If a lizard feels it is in danger, it will hiss at you like a cat.

These lizards do not have strong enough venom to kill a healthy person. Their bites are very painful, though, and the lizards hold on tightly. If you are bitten by a Gila monster or a Mexican beaded lizard, you should call 911 and see a doctor. If you see one of these lizards, leave it alone and let it hide.

GLOSSARY

aggressive (uh-GREH-siv) Ready to fight.

burrows (BUR-ohz) Holes an animal digs to live in.

defend (dih-FEND) To guard from harm.

endangered (in-DAYN-jerd) In danger of dying out.

family (FAM-lee) The scientific name for a large group of plants or animals that are alike in some ways.

glands (GLANDZ) Parts of the body that make something to help with a bodily function.

habitats (HA-beh-tats) The kinds of land where an animal or a plant naturally lives.

hibernate (HY-bur-nayt) To spend the winter in a sleeplike state.

mate (MAYT) To get together to make babies.

predators (PREH-duh-terz) Animals that kill other animals for food.

saliva (suh-LY-vuh) The stuff in the mouth that starts to break down food and helps food slide down the throat.

species (SPEE-sheez) One kind of living thing. All people are one species.

temperature (TEM-pur-cher) The heat in a living body.

venomous (VEH-nuh-mus) Having a poisonous bite.

INDEX

B
burrows, 12

D
desert(s), 10, 18

G
Gila River, 8
glands, 16

H
habitat(s), 10, 20

J
jaws, 16

P
predators, 12

S
saliva, 16, 20
scales, 6, 8
snake(s), 6, 16
species, 8, 10

V
venom, 4, 16, 20

WEB SITES

Due to the changing nature of Internet links, PowerKids Press has developed an online list of Web sites related to the subject of this book. This site is updated regularly. Please use this link to access the list:
www.powerkidslinks.com/poi/dliz/